LITTLE CHILDREN BIG EXAMS

FROM ONE PARENT TO ANOTHER

AYSE GUNDUZ SEVIN

MAGNUS EDUCATION

LONDON

Magnus Education London
16 Bowerdean Street
London SW6 3TW

www.magnuseducationlondon.co.uk

First Edition

A catalogue record of this book is available from the
British Library

ISBN 978-0-9957326-0-5

Cover design by Paul Mumby

Layout and page design by Sahin Gumus at Creamis Media

*This book is dedicated to
my beloved mother, Aysun Gunduz.
I have always felt her support even on my worst
days and she has always surprised me by being
extremely calm whenever I expected her to panic.*

CONTENTS

ACKNOWLEDGEMENTS

I would like to thank my friend Aysegul Ozcan for her endless energy to keep me on the track while I was writing this book and my husband, Teoman Sevin, for encouraging and supporting me in everything I want to do in life.

AUTHOR'S NOTE

I am not only a career woman, but also a mum who has put a lot of thought, effort and energy into my children's well-being; socially, emotionally and academically. I have noticed that, in the UK, as soon as two mums get together, they automatically start talking about one of these three subjects; current schools, future schools or exams. Obviously, mothers are very concerned about their offspring's academic lives. As a mum, currently going through the system with two boys with completely different characters, I believe I have accumulated some solid insights into the system.

I wanted to write this book because if I could have found this kind of experience-based information myself, with clear resources, I would have benefited from it a great deal. But I couldn't.

If you are taking the time to read this book, it means that you and your children are very lucky. You have concerns, but your concerns are privileged concerns. Because you are reading this to make sure your children get the best education and have better lives. Whereas in the world, even today, there are so many children who still need the basics in life such as food and safe shelter. The realities of life always helped me to put things into perspective. Therefore, I am donating ten per cent of the royalties from this book to Save the Children that runs world-class programmes to save children's lives and challenge world leaders to keep to their promises to give children a brighter future. I appreciate their efforts and I would like an opportunity to contribute to their work. When you buy this book, you won't only be benefitting your own children, but also other kids who are very vulnerable.

Thank you.

MY REASONS FOR WRITING THIS BOOK

When your first child is born, you think that you will never have another uninterrupted sleep in your life again. But as other parents told us so many times, they really grow up very quickly. That means the issues you have to address change continuously also.

As a parent, choosing a school for your child is one of the most important decisions you are going to make. Your child will spend a significant amount of time at school and his teachers and school friends will become a big part of not only his but also your daily life.

In the UK, the search for a school for your child starts as soon as you learn you are pregnant. If the parents are not familiar with the system, the process can be overwhelming.

It is easier if you have family and friends around you who have already gone along a similar path and would like to share their experiences with you. But, unfortunately, not everybody is surrounded by this kind of network. Also, some people may choose not to follow the same path and prefer to find out what works best for their families themselves.

I love talking to my friends and family and learn from their successes and failures. But I also like to learn from people who might have different, or sometimes more academic, backgrounds and experiences. Therefore, while I was raising my children, I read every book I could find at the book stores. They were not only about raising a child physically and emotionally but also academically. I learnt a lot from the good ones, and I learnt at least couple of things from the poor ones too.

My journey started nine months before Sarp was born. Since then, I have read numerous books and I have shared my feelings and concerns with so many great mums.

Other mums and books have been the greatest support for me in raising my children. By writing this book I want to share my positive and negative experiences with other parents through the most effective method that worked for me, a book.

CHAPTER 1

Good News

It was seven fifteen in the morning. The phone started ringing. I was still in bed.

We had moved to São Paulo, Brazil, ten days previously from London and the new school the kids were going to go to was still on Carnival break. My husband was already at work. The children and I were sleeping.

I got up and went to the living room to find my phone. I saw my husband's name on the screen and answered the call.

"Come on, wake up! Your son has got an offer from Westminster School and you are still sleeping!"

I froze. Have I heard right? I thought to myself.

In the meantime, Teoman was talking about an email, the headmaster of Dulwich Prep London (DPL), had sent.

I immediately checked my email and saw the word 'Congratulations'. So it was true.

I was speechless. I don't remember what else we talked about but, when I hung up, my mind was blank.

I allowed myself a few minutes to let the news sink in, then I went to the room where Sarp was asleep. Usually, it takes some time and effort to wake him up.

I whispered to him very lightly; "You got into Westminster."

He immediately opened his eyes and looked at me.

He said, "What?" in a very low voice.

CHAPTER 2

Choosing a Prep School

L et's go back in time.

In 2001, I moved to London from Istanbul, Turkey, to work for Citigroup as a private banker.

Two years later, I had my son, Sarp. I was thirty-one-years-old.

Even when I was pregnant, some people asked me which schools I had in my mind or if I had registered my unborn child with any nurseries. I just smiled at them. I thought they were overly concerned about everything and did not have anything else to do.

When Sarp was one-year-old, my husband and I arranged for my mum to come from Istanbul all the way to London to look after Sarp, so that we could go to the Maldives for a week. Before our holiday, I realised that I had no idea about schools and the education system in England and bought a book called The Good Schools Guide to read on holiday. I took it with me to the Maldives.

On the first morning of our holiday, we had a very nice breakfast and went to the beach. We swam in the lagoon with thousands of colourful fish. It was amazing.

Then, we lay down on the beach and talked about how lovely it was to be alone again without thinking about nappies and bottles. After a while, both my husband and I took out our books and started to read.

The problem was that the book I was reading was very depressing. Firstly, I noticed that a few schools had already closed their registration for my son's entry year to nursery and, secondly, I saw that most of the good schools assess kids before offering them a place. This meant that Sarp needed to be assessed when he was a little over two-years-old to be accepted by a nursery when he was three.

I joked about taking the first flight back immediately and registering Sarp at nurseries. It was a joke but, at the same time, there was some truth in it. I was in a panic.

During that holiday, I took the task seriously and studied my lesson really well. I examined all the possible schools in the book and I understood that schools offer, and value, different things and I must find the school that was right for me and for my son.

Firstly, I made a list of things that were important for me.

1. I wanted a reputable and good academic school.

2. I wanted a school that started at the age of three.

I noticed that some schools start at the age of three and others at the age of four. Being a working mum, I preferred my son to spend his time at school in an active environment rather than sitting at home with his nanny and watching TV.

3. I wanted a school that provided the longest possible education before Sarp needed to take any formal exams.

After reading the book, I noticed that the schooling system in the UK is very complicated and paved with exams and assessments at different stages, starting from a very early age. So, I immediately understood that I wanted a school that wouldn't put any exam pressure on me and my son for a long time.

4. I wanted a school that was close to our house.

That was a very big problem because we were living in Canada Water, a newly developed area with no established, good prep schools.

When I returned from holiday, I immediately phoned the schools I was interested in and asked for prospectuses and registration forms. Even though I wasn't interested in them, just out of curiosity, I called a couple of those schools that I was supposed to register my son with before he was born, to see if it was really true. And it was! Their registrations were closed for my son's entry year.

Finally, I decided on Dulwich Prep London (DPL). It was an academic school that started at the age of three and continued until thirteen. I also discovered that, even though DPL and Dulwich College are separate schools, the kids from DPL were not having much difficulty in getting a place at Dulwich College when they reached thirteen.

The second step was to prepare my one-year-old son for an assessment that I had no idea about. Basically, I couldn't do anything because there is nothing you can do to prepare a one-year-old child for an exam or assessment.

Apart from that we had couple of other issues too.

First of all, we are a Turkish family living in London and we have always made an effort to speak in Turkish at home. Sarp's nanny was the only person who spoke to him in English. Because of him being exposed to two languages, Sarp started to speak when he was two-years-old. By the time he was called for the assessment, he could speak neither Turkish nor English properly.

Although he couldn't talk much, he was a very playful child. From a really early age, he loved doing puzzles and looking at books.

At the time of his assessment, he was obsessed with construction machines and his favourite object was a book about diggers. Even though he could not speak properly, he knew the names of all the parts of diggers and he was very willing to tell you about them.

The second issue was that he wasn't toilet trained yet. I did everything possible to get rid of the nappy before the assessment but he simply wasn't ready for that. And, in the end, I relaxed and thought that if someone is assessing a two-year-old boy, that person should be prepared for nappies.

My third concern was that Sarp was born on 25 August. In England the cut-off date for the academic year is 31 August. So my son was probably going to be the youngest, and least mature, in his year.

Years later, I learnt that some parents whose children were born very close to the cut-off date held their kids back for one year so that when they started school the following year, they were the oldest and most mature in their year group. Then, of course, they are the ones who start reading and writing first because their brains are more developed and they are the ones who usually get into the school teams for football, rugby, swimming etc because, basically, they are physically more able. For further reading on this subject check out a book called Outliers by Malcolm Gladwell. If I had known this earlier I would have definitely held Sarp back for a year.

Anyway, one week before the assessment, Sarp got sick. He continuously had a very high temperature and couldn't get out of bed for days. On the assessment day, he was better but still in need of Calpol to keep his temperature under control.

On the big day, my husband and I were very nervous. We went to the assessment with Sarp's favourite digger book. I still remember how little and cute he was with his honey-coloured, curly hair and big, bluish-green eyes, dressed in the dark blue sweater he was wearing to make him look smart.

He didn't have any separation anxiety. He happily went away to another room with the lady who was going to assess him.

After thirty minutes, he was brought back. The assessor asked us what language he spoke. Sarp hadn't spoken a word of English during the assessment. The lady who assessed Sarp told us that she hadn't understood anything he was saying but he was a very happy child.

We went back home and rewound that moment in our minds so many times. My husband thought that the comment was not positive but for me it sounded like it was. Basically, we were clueless about what to expect.

One day, almost a month later, I came home early from work. I opened the door and saw a couple of envelopes that had been pushed through the letter box waiting for me inside on the floor. I immediately recognised the red stamp belonging to DPL on one of the envelopes. I opened it in a state of terror. I saw the word 'Congratulations'. Sarp had been offered a place. I started crying.

You can't believe how happy I was. I immediately called my husband, then my mum and shared the good news with them. Later on, I learnt that after my conversation with my mum she called her neighbours and friends and told them too. That day, we were a very happy and proud family. And the reason was my son had been accepted by a nursery!

I was so relieved that I didn't need to worry about exams and assessments any more until Sarp was thirteen-years-old. It felt like an incredibly long time. How wrong I was!

CHAPTER 3

Early School Days

S arp loved his school. It was a good choice. But, of course, I had couple of issues.

First of all, I was a full-time working mum. I could not mix with other mums since our nanny did all the school runs and I could rarely go to school shows and assemblies. The truth is, by the time I realised that assemblies were something parents were supposed to attend, I had already missed a lot of them.

Also, when I was choosing that school my Turkish side had told me that half an hour drive was nothing. In Istanbul it usually takes at least one hour, sometimes even more to get to work or school. But then I wasn't aware of the whole play date concept.

I noticed that, in England, schools require a serious amount of parental involvement. This is not a big issue because, no matter how well educated women are, as soon as they have a baby, the majority of them prefer to quit working. Probably, it is because childcare is very expensive and grandparents either don't live close by or they prefer not to be involved in looking after their grandchildren.

That means all those very well-educated and competitive ex-lawyers, bankers and consultants etc divert their full energy to their children. So there is no limit to the support or push kids can get from their mums academically and socially. Mums' diaries are always full with play dates and after school activities such as; swimming, tennis, karate, chess, football, rugby, ballet, dance, drama, gymnastics, piano, arts and crafts, circus skills and much more, just you name it! When you want to arrange a play date you usually get a date in two to three weeks' time.

Of course, living so far away from school, and with me being a working mum, it was not very easy to arrange play dates. Luckily, there was one other boy who lived in our area and had a working mum so we understood each other's problems and managed to organise play dates without much effort. Even now, the boys are the best of friends.

I would definitely encourage you not to make the same mistake as I did and to choose a school which is close to where you live.

CHAPTER 4

Derin

The year Sarp started nursery, I became pregnant for the second time and, nine months later, we had our second son, Derin. Sarp and Derin were four years apart.

Sarp and Derin had very different childhoods. I don't think one has had a better childhood than the other, they were just different.

The reason we moved to London was for work and we had no one from our families living in the UK. As a pregnant woman, with no experience in childcare, and with no one to get help from, I read every possible book on childcare. There are a few authors who are legends in childcare such as Gina Ford and Annabel Karmel and I benefited from their books vastly, even though I only chose to apply the parts that I found suitable for me and my sons.

When we were raising Sarp, we did everything according to the books. When Sarp was a baby, he had a very structured routine. Every day he went out twice for fresh air. His nanny played with him all day long. They did puzzles, they played games. They read books. They watched TV together; CBBC of course. And again, when my husband and I came home from work, our main job was to spend time with Sarp and, again, to play with him. We had a bedtime routine and, every evening since he was born, either my husband or I have read to him.

Whereas when Derin was born four years later, I was an experienced mum. I knew what to worry about and what not to worry about. So, I was much more relaxed. I had also experienced everything the books told me to do first hand with Sarp and I knew which strategies to apply and which ones to ignore.

I could also see how difficult it was for Sarp to have a sibling and start to share his parents with the newcomer. Suddenly, in one day, he became the older brother and everybody expected him to be more mature. He was only four-years-old. So, even though Derin was the younger one, when I came home from work, I always tried to spend a lot of time with Sarp to make sure he didn't feel left out.

Thirdly, when Derin was seven months old, I had to go back to work. Just before having Derin I had changed my job. My new company was aware of the fact that I was pregnant when they hired me and I felt that it wouldn't have been fair to them if I had extended my maternity leave to twelve months.

The school was a long way from our house and, since I was back at work, our nanny had to do all the school runs with Derin, which left him with barely enough time to eat and sleep. He had to spend a significant amount of time in the car and almost had no time to play or read at home. He couldn't go out to the park twice a day to feed the ducks. Almost all day he was in the car going back and forth to Dulwich.

My children's characters and interests are very different too. Derin had a very high EQ. He was very intelligent and receptive emotionally, and always knew what was going on around him, but he didn't show much interest in books or puzzles.

All these things added up and, as a result, I had a completely different experience with Derin in the process of getting into nursery.

CHAPTER 5

Derin's Assessment

In the UK, some schools have sibling priority which means that, if you have a child studying at that school, your other kids will automatically be offered places. Of course, DPL, being an academic school, didn't have sibling priority which meant that Derin had to go via the same route as Sarp four years earlier and had to be assessed when he was two-years-old. Derin was born on 29 July and, like Sarp, he was again very young for his year group.

The first problem with the assessment was that Derin hadn't started speaking yet. Neither in English, nor in Turkish. Of course, he was saying a few things but not enough for him to pass the assessment.

Also, he didn't like sitting down and playing with toys either. He preferred to follow Sarp and us in the house and passed his time at home without doing any focused play.

When the day of the assessment came, my husband and I took Derin to Dulwich Prep Nursery. The way the school assessed the kids had changed in the past four years. In Sarp's time, it was an individual assessment but, I guess, because the number of applicants had increased they had started to hold group assessments.

All the children were taken to a big room and their anxious parents were left behind trying to socialise with one another. After ten minutes, one of the assessors came into the room and walked towards us. I immediately felt that something was wrong. She asked us if Derin could speak at all. I remember us giving vague answers to that question. We tried to emphasise how nervous Derin was with the process. She then went back to the assessment room again, leaving us feeling very worried.

The funny thing was, when Derin came out of the assessment, he told us with his limited language skills that it was a good school and he liked it there.

This time, I knew for sure that the assessment hadn't gone well. And one month later, when we got the letter, I saw that the result was indeed, not good.

CHAPTER 6

A Little Bit About Myself

Now I would like to tell you a little bit about my personality.

I am usually very content with what I have and I don't ask for a lot of things. But when something is really important to me, I do everything necessary. If it doesn't happen, despite all my efforts, it doesn't happen, but I make sure I do everything possible.

I believe, to get what you want, you must also be lucky. Sometimes, you do everything in your capacity and it still doesn't happen. But I also believe that when the luck presents itself, you should have done all the preparation beforehand and you should be in a position to grab that luck.

CHAPTER 7

Strong Will

With your firstborn, you look at every possible school and you try to choose the best one for your child. With your second child, convenience plays a big role. Even though they are very different, if they are the same sex, you just assume that they will go to the same school and if they are not, you try to find a good school which is also convenient for the other one. Therefore, it was very important for me to send Derin to DPL too.

After getting the rejection letter, I waited for a week. Then, I called the school and asked them if there was anyone who was not going to accept the offer. Of course, it was too early to know that and I was told to give them a call in a couple of months' time. In the meantime, I registered Derin at another nursery to make sure he was at least going to be prepared for the next year's assessment.

I waited for one month and called the school again. The answer was still negative. I didn't mind. When you know that there is nothing you can lose, there is no harm in trying. So, one month before the schools started, I contacted the school again.

That year the school had decided to start part-time afternoon sessions for the first time. The hours were very awkward and, of course, in the end, some of the parents whose kids got a place in that session decided to decline their place.

I was told to bring Derin back for another assessment. We were so excited about this second chance and we tried our best to prepare Derin in our limited two-day period. In the meantime, Derin's speaking skills had also improved.

When the day came, the headmistress of the nursery welcomed us and took Derin to another room to assess him. The headmistress had come to DPL from another local school a few months previously. To our horror, she came back five minutes later and told us that Derin was not cooperating and it might be a good idea to do the assessment when we were in the room too.

She showed Derin a flash card with an elephant

on it and asked him what it was. No answer, Derin stood still.

He was shown a few more cards and each time it was silence again. I didn't know what to do. I knew that Derin knew everything on those cards and this time he could really speak properly but he chose not to talk. He wasn't even three yet.

At one stage, he was shown a card with a pair of scissors on it and Derin looked at me and then at the headmistress and made a very slow, cutting-like, hand gesture.

I knew I had to do something and I knew I had to do it quickly.

I started saying that he spoke fine at home. He knew all of the images on the flash cards but he was very nervous with the process. At the same time the headmistress said that it was a shame, but it wasn't possible for her to offer Derin a place at the nursery.

I heard her but I kept repeating that Derin spoke very well at home and, if necessary, I could bring a reference from his nursery about how well he could speak. I added that he knew everything he was being asked but didn't want to talk just then, which was completely true.

Meanwhile, she kept repeating that Derin was not

ready and it wasn't possible for her to offer him a place.

I kept going, saying how much we loved the school, how happy my other son was there and that we really wanted Derin to go to the school also.

There came a point when there was nothing else the headmistress could say. But at the same time, she noticed that we weren't going anywhere. I kept on saying the same things over and over again in a very polite manner.

Finally, she said that she was going to talk to Sarp's teacher regarding how well he was doing at school and, if the reference was good, she would offer Derin a place.

That afternoon, we received a phone call from the school and the headmistress congratulated us and welcomed Derin to DPL.

Although what I did was extremely embarrassing, for me it was one of the most important achievements in my life. Also, when I think about the whole process, I feel that if they're not embarrassed about assessing a two-year-old child, still in nappies, I shouldn't be ashamed for what I had done either.

This was my personal method to get my younger son into the same school as his brother. But to achieve this result, there is also another, less embarrassing, method with more chance of success. It is not for everyone, but again it is worth the hassle if you have a little bit of free time.

You should be prepared to devote some of your time and energy to your chosen school. To me, it doesn't seem like an easy option for full-time working mums but, of course, it depends on the mum.

I think the most effective method is to work voluntarily for the Parent Teacher Association (PTA). If the PTA meets too often, you are not capable of coping with the tasks required or you don't want to be involved with personal clashes between ambitious women, then you can opt for helping casually in classroom activities when parents' help is needed and accompanying pupils to museums, picnics etc on school trips. All of these activities not only help to increase your visibility at the school, but also that of your child.

In practice, of course, the most efficient method is working for the PTA. Because then, you are not only visible to class teachers, but also to the headmasters and headmistresses and, when the time comes, it is very difficult to reject the child of someone who has devoted so much time and energy to the school.

Also, lately, changes in regulations have meant that parents' involvement in school has become more limited and restricted.

To me, this is like discovering the same truth again, this time from an adult perspective. I remember from my own childhood that the kids whose mums worked for the PTA at our school always got the better roles in school shows. My mum was a working mum, like me, and she never had the time or will to do that but even then, as a child, I had noticed how rewarding it was for the children whose parents were involved in school affairs.

At the same time, I don't want you to get me wrong. If I were in a position to decide which child to accept and which to decline, I would do the same. I am only speaking from my experience but, if there is nothing wrong with the child, the children whose parents are involved with their school would have at least the same chance of doing well at school, socially and academically, than the other ones, if not more.

CHAPTER 8

Kumon

One day, I was talking to one of my colleagues at work. She has three daughters and told me that her youngest one had got into St Paul's Girls' School. I knew it was very difficult to get into that school and I never thought that my sons could have a chance in those kinds of schools when their mum spoke English with such a strong accent. But then I thought, if my Singaporean friend's daughter could manage to do it, her accent was not great either, why not my sons? I knew that there were also two very famous boys' schools in London, namely Westminster and St Paul's schools. I knew about Eton too, but as a Turkish mum I couldn't even think about sending my children to a boarding school.

Me being a very competitive mum, I immediately asked my friend how she managed to get her daughter into St Paul's and what extra preparation was needed.

Then I heard about Kumon for the first time in my life. It is a system that was set up by a Japanese man called Kumon to help kids with English and maths in their local language in different countries. It is available in almost every country in the world. The system is based on children doing a certain amount of work every day. Students can start Kumon at any age, even as young as two-years-old.

There are Kumon centres in England and sessions usually take place in church halls. Firstly, call your local Kumon Centre and tell them that you are interested and book an assessment session for your child to go there and do a test in English or maths, or both. It takes around forty minutes, depending on how fast your child works.

Then you are given a one week supply of Kumon worksheets which are little bit easier than your child's current level to make sure the foundation is strong. Once a week your child is expected to go to the centre to do that day's worksheets there, to hand in the previous week's work and to receive the next week's supply. To follow the child's progress, the work he/she has done is noted and at the end of the session your child is rewarded with a candy.

In theory, it doesn't sound bad. I thought that doing little bit of work every day would help Sarp to gain good studying habits and also help him to improve academically.

So we started Kumon.

Sarp was then seven-years-old.

First of all, when I say 'certain amount of work every day', I really mean it. There is no holiday, no weekend, no Christmas, nothing, 365 days a year. And when I say 'certain amount of work', it means twenty, A5 pages of maths or English, or both. That means the child needs to do around 200 maths questions every day. The questions are very repetitive. So the child is expected to answer the same questions over and over again. Obviously, if a child does 200 additions every day for one month, he/she ends up knowing the answer without even thinking.

Sarp instantly hated it. It was supposed to take fifteen minutes every day but it usually took at least one hour, sometimes an hour and a half. There were a few reasons for that. Firstly, he didn't want to do it, so I spent at least half an hour trying to convince him, bribe him even, to sit down and start doing his Kumon.

Secondly, even after he started doing it, he didn't work quickly, he frequently stopped to complain and moan. Thirdly, in the beginning, even if he was concentrating and focused, he was slow in answering the questions and there were so many questions to answer.

It was a very difficult thing to do but, at the same time, I knew that, academically, it was beneficial too. Even after a very short period I started to see tangible results. At school he started to get extension works in maths and English. Also, he knew academically he was better than most of the kids in his class and that gave him confidence.

While he was doing better and better at school, our clashes at home were getting out of control. Every day I was coming home from work tired and finding myself in a battle.

For me, it was very difficult to give it up when I saw Sarp benefiting from Kumon even though he hated it. So I managed to carry on for five months.

At the end of this time, the atmosphere in our house was unbearable. Sarp's behaviour had deteriorated significantly. He didn't want to go to school. Every morning he woke up with excuses not to go.

I knew there was something wrong with his school

life. So I went to the school and talked to his teacher. She told me that Sarp was doing very well academically and he was more advanced than the others in his class, therefore, he was not interested in class learning and, instead of listening to his teacher and joining the activities, he would chit chat with other kids and continuously distract the class. Because of that he was often told off.

On top of that he started to have tics!

I panicked. I read everything on the Internet about tics and found out, not surprisingly, that they were a sign of distress.

There is a huge difference between your child telling you that he hates doing something and you seeing the effect of this on him physically.

I felt so guilty for harming my son only to teach him to add up faster. So what? Everybody learns how to read and write and do maths. I kept asking myself, "Was it worth it? Am I happy now?"

I gave up Kumon immediately. From that moment on, things got better and better every day. I still made sure Sarp was doing his homework properly but that was it. His behaviour improved immediately. My mood improved immediately too. Our house stopped being a battle arena and became a proper home again. Everybody was relaxed and happy.

This was my first major mistake as a mum.

But I don't want you to misunderstand me. In our experience, Kumon didn't work well for us but I am not saying that the system is a complete failure. Actually, it is a very good system but you should be careful about how to apply it. At a later stage in my life, I went back to Kumon and tried it again with my younger son, Derin, and it worked brilliantly. I will talk about this later in the book. I just want you to realise that the most important thing is to know how to benefit from different resources and materials without letting them dominate your life.

CHAPTER 9

My Childhood

At this point, I think I should tell you a little bit about myself and my childhood.

My father was a lawyer. When he married my mum he was twenty-eight and she was eighteen-years-old. My mum had just graduated from high school and had taken the exams for university. When my father proposed, she wanted to marry him but also told him that she wanted to go back to university at some stage. They got married. My mum got pregnant soon after and they had my brother, Onur.

In the beginning, they moved from one place to another and lived in small villages for a few years. Then they returned back to Eskisehir, a medium sized city in the middle part of Turkey where their families lived.

When my brother was seven-years-old, he started

going to primary school at the same time my mum started going to university. Her great-grandfather was a pharmacist and my mum had spent her childhood flicking through his handwritten books about plants and being fascinated by them. Of course, when it was time to decide what she was going to study, without even thinking, she wanted to be a pharmacist.

During her second year at university, she was pregnant again. This time they had a daughter and that was me! Even though she had a lot of difficulties along the way, with determination she managed to overcome these and graduated four years later. She started working immediately.

I had a very easy-going childhood. I played on the streets with my friends all day long without anyone trying to teach me anything. It was all free play. There were kids of all ages and we all played together. The older ones took care of the younger ones and the younger ones respected and trusted the older ones.

When I was seven-years-old, I started primary school. Like my sons, I was one of the youngest in my year. On the first day of school, I noticed that all the other kids knew how to write their names and surnames in the class, except me.

Towards the end of the first year, my teacher invited my parents to school and told them that I was the only one in the class who hadn't learnt how to read yet.

My dad decided to help me at home and, at the end of the first month, I was at completely the same level as my friends at school. After that I never looked back. Academically, I always did well.

In Turkey, to get into academically selective senior schools, we used to take a common entrance exam when we were eleven-years-old. The kids who were not successful in those exams continued at their usual high schools. In my case, there was only one academically selective senior school in our city and I was going to try for that one school. Of course, with me being the youngest in my class, I was still ten-years-old.

All the kids who came from similar backgrounds to me started to prepare for this exam. As usual, tutoring was the biggest part of it.

My mum found a tutor for me too. I went to the tutor's house for the first lesson. I still remember that lesson today and how clueless I was about the questions he was asking.

That day, when I came back home, I had a rash

and my body was covered with itchy, red spots. My mum looked at me and she said, "It is not worth it! You are not going there again." And that was it. I took the exam later on and, of course, I failed.

That year, another significant thing happened in my life. My father passed away. He had a stroke. He was only forty-nine-years-old.

When I look back, I remember those days very clearly. The house was full of people. My mum was very sad, not only because she had lost her husband, but also she was very worried about the life in front of her with two children, one eleven, the other nineteen. She was only thirty-nine-years-old herself.

My grandma took me to my mum's bedroom and told me the bad news. I remember having a long, good cry on top of my mum's bed.

But kids are strange creatures. I also remember that a few days later there was supposed to be a Tarzan movie on TV and I really wanted to watch it. When that day came, the house was still very crowded and we hadn't started watching TV yet. I went to my grandmother and told her about the movie. She was a very wise woman and I loved her dearly. She immediately solved my problem. She sent me to my best friend Reyhan's flat. They lived on the top floor of our building. I recall watching that movie there very happily.

This reminds me that there is one thing we should always keep in our minds. Kids really live in the now. I know this from my own experiences as a child.

Up until that point, I had a very easy childhood. You would think that after my father's death, things would have changed dramatically. This is not true either.

There had been some changes but, in general, my life continued as usual. My mum was very caring and soft but, at the same time, a no-nonsense woman. She was a contented person.

I continued to be a very good-natured child. I always did well at school. I decided when to study, how to study, how much to study and no one ever checked my homework. I usually got seven or eight out of ten in exams and my mum neither exaggerated my success by offering prizes or gifts nor asked me to study more and do better.

I have one memory that will give you an insight to my mum's character. When I was in middle school, I had an English exam and English was not my favourite subject. When the results were announced I learnt that I got two out of ten.

Up until that point, I had never got such a bad mark. I was devastated. When I came home, I told my mum about it. I was so upset. She looked at me and told me, "Now you are a real student, you deserve a gift for that." And she bought me a very beautiful, green jumper which I adored and wore for years.

When the time came for university exam preparation, she told me that it is important for a woman to have a career. Life is full of surprises and a woman should be able to stand on her own feet. This time she found the best two tutors in our city and paid a fortune to them. But again, she left all the decisions to me on when, how, or how much I studied. She always trusted me.

When the exam results were announced, I learnt that I had got into Istanbul Technical University Textile Engineering, which was the same university my brother had graduated from. It was among the top three universities in Turkey then. My mum was delighted with the result and that year we moved to Istanbul together.

CHAPTER 10

Holiday Catch Up

I had given up Kumon completely and focused on extracurricular activities and homework during term times. During the holidays, I always found activities to stimulate the kids physically, mentally and academically. Such as tennis, swimming, drama, movies, children's theatre, lots of play dates and Bond exercise books in Maths, English, Verbal and Non-Verbal Reasoning.

Sarp had a much more positive attitude towards Bond exercise books compared to Kumon. There were a few reasons for that. One of them was that I only asked him to do those extra exercises when it was holiday time. So he knew that he had a whole day in front of him to be with his friends, play computer games or go to the park for football.

The second reason was, every day I only asked him to do one test each, from two different subjects of his choice. Sarp could easily finish the tests in a maximum of half an hour. Sometimes they only took ten to fifteen minutes, depending on the subjects he chose. So they didn't take Sarp a long time.

The third reason was the format. Kumon worksheets and Bond exercise books were very different. In Kumon, until you reach a certain level it is expected that you will excel in basics, such as sums, take away, division, multiplication, fractions etc. You are supposed to do thousands of them before moving to the next level and they are very repetitive. Up until a certain point, there is no problem-solving. Whereas Bond books focus on problem-solving. Sarp found that less boring.

Years later, I learned that, each year, the school tests kids to measure their ability in maths, English, verbal and non-verbal reasoning. And Sarp was scoring very highly in those tests.

Apparently, when the time comes to think about which schools to choose at 11+ or 13+, schools take these results into account when recommending the suitable schools for the child. So, in a way,

Sarp was prepared for those tests without me even knowing it.

CHAPTER 11

Don't Panic!

Sarp was in Year 4. He was almost nine-years-old. Even though he was one of the youngest, he was doing well academically and socially.

We had moved to Fulham from Canada Water two years earlier. I had chosen Fulham, even though moving to Dulwich made much more sense. I think it is in human nature to make repetitive and deliberate mistakes!

I had quit my job and started doing the school runs. I had much more interaction with other mums and knew what was going on at school.

Towards the end of the year, I noticed that mums started chatting about future school alternatives. Some of them had older kids and they were experienced with the process.

Initially, the conversations didn't make any sense

to me at all. Because I knew that DPL was a school that continued until the age of thirteen. For me, it was too early to start talking about future schools and exams.

I was so wrong!

A couple of weeks later, the school sent a letter inviting all Year 4 parents for an informative evening talk about future schools. My husband and I went to the talk. Our headmaster had prepared a very nice presentation and on the first slide was written 'DON'T PANIC' in bold letters. Of course, as soon as I saw that I thought I should start panicking.

I learnt that some very selective schools have their own pretests at eleven. If the child is successful in these tests, he is offered a conditional place to start the school when he is thirteen-years-old. The condition is that they pass the Common Entrance (CE) tests in Year 8 with the minimum mark required by that school.

We were given a list of all the major schools in the UK. On the list there were deadlines for registrations and exam dates. Some of the registration deadlines were quite early and some of the schools didn't have any pretests at all.

One of the schools that didn't do pretesting was

Dulwich College. The main reason I had chosen DPL for Sarp in the beginning was its informal ties with Dulwich College. I knew that it was a very good school and, for boys coming from DPL, it wasn't very difficult to get into. So if we decided Sarp should go there, we didn't need to worry about tests until he was in Year 8.

The headmaster told us that the school would arrange one to one meetings with parents to discuss which schools would be suitable for their children. He also suggested that parents start visiting schools with their kids and make a shortlist of those that they are interested in starting the registration process for.

After the meeting, mums' playground talk during pick-ups was mainly concentrated on this subject.

I noticed that families had different approaches on how to select the schools for their kids.

Traditional approach

English parents are very well-informed about the schools and the processes. Usually, mums and dads come from single sex, boarding schools and if their child is a boy he is expected to go to his dad's school or if it is a girl, she is expected to go to her mum's school.

Kid-centred approach

Parents really try to maximise their child's happiness and potential by choosing the right school for them. If the kid is sporty they choose schools that take sport seriously with big green grounds and lots of sport facilities. If their child is arty, they choose schools based on how well the school is doing in art. If the kid is musical, they choose the schools accordingly. The actual school building, how much light it gets, the size of the school's grounds are very important.

Convenience based approach

Most of the kids at DPL live in the Dulwich area and it is very convenient for parents if their kids to go to Dulwich College. It is also a very good school.

Social network based approach

Even though some parents do not come from boarding schools themselves, they are aware of the advantages of belonging to an elite social group that takes care of one another later in life, especially during their careers. So they want their children to go to a boarding school that could provide a social network for them at a later stage.

Academic and reputable school approach

Some parents only search for the most academic

and reputable schools and, even before they go and visit the school to find out if it is suitable for their child, they start preparing their children for those schools' exams.

Usually, these kinds of parents were not born in England but moved here because of job opportunities. They come from cultures that value academic achievement highly; mainly Chinese, Indian, Russian and Turkish. Even though I try to resist the urge, I am definitely in this group.

CHAPTER 12

Choosing a Senior School for Sarp

We are a Turkish family and, in Turkey, boarding schools are not common at all. For us, boarding school was not an option. Sarp was a boy who always enjoyed being at home and, thank God, when the time came for him to decide, he didn't want to go to a boarding school.

Also, we were not ready for him to leave us either. Even though I asked him unbiasedly if he would have considered going to a boarding school, luckily, he said he had no intention of going to one. If he wanted to go, probably we would have done everything possible to change his mind anyway.

That decision left us with London day schools only.

In London, there are many good, established, reputable schools with different characteristics and locations.

Within those, Westminster School and St Paul's School are the most famous, reputable and most difficult to get into.

Then comes King's College School Wimbledon. The school offers both A Levels and International Baccalaureate in the sixth form. It is as difficult as the other two, or maybe more so, to get into. During my visit I could tell that the school values academic achievement highly.

Then there is City of London School. This is a new and upcoming school, located in the heart of the City and very convenient for people who live in the south. People who work in the City like this school a lot because of its convenience but it doesn't have much in the way of grounds.

Initially, I thought that it would be easier to get into City of London School compared to Westminster, St Paul's and King's College Wimbledon schools but, actually, its exam was very difficult and a few kids who did very well in other schools' exams and interviews couldn't even pass the exam stage there.

The other option for me was, of course, Dulwich College. Actually, it was the school I was most impressed with, after attending all the school visits and information evenings. The students were very down to earth. The school had a great feel and its grounds and facilities were amazing.

I knew that The Latymer School was also very good but, somehow, I thought that instead of Latymer, Sarp could go to Dulwich College, so I didn't research that school at all.

CHAPTER 13

Different Opinions

My husband and I had to make our minds up quickly about which schools to apply to. This wasn't easy because we had different opinions. I wanted Sarp to try to get into Westminster or St Paul's schools. Whereas my husband, coming from the best academic schools throughout all of his education, including boarding school which is very rare in Turkey, thought that the school we chose should be established, reputable and academically good, but not necessarily the most academic one. He wanted Sarp to continue with Dulwich College.

St Paul's School had a very early registration date and we had to decide quickly. So, I arranged an appointment with the school to discuss the potential alternatives for Sarp.

In our meeting, we were told that the suitable

schools for Sarp were Westminster and St Paul's. We had already mentioned that we were not interested in boarding schools. Otherwise, Eton and Winchester were options for Sarp too.

My husband and I felt very proud but, at the same time, I was also concerned. I knew from my playground chats that, in previous years, many parents had been advised to apply to top academic schools for their children but, of course, in the end some of the kids couldn't get into them. So I asked for back up schools too. Then King's College School Wimbledon and City of London schools were suggested to us. All four of them had pretests at the age of eleven. Our last back up school was Dulwich College which didn't have a pretest. If Sarp couldn't get into one of those four schools, he could still try for Dulwich College when he was in Year 8.

In the meeting I also asked if we should get extra help to prepare Sarp for the exams. By extra help, I meant private tutoring, of course, and we were told that there was no need, as the school does all the necessary preparation, mock exams and interview practices.

We said, "Thank you." And left the meeting.

It was so good to hear from someone else that

our son was good enough academically for these schools but, at the same time, it was scary. Even if you aim for the schools that are the hardest to get into, there is a big possibility that your child will fail after all their hard work and effort.

CHAPTER 14

Feeder Schools

The headmaster or headmistress of your child's current school is one of the most important people in the admission process for senior schools.

As a parent you must definitely work on this together with your current headmaster.

First of all, he must genuinely think that your son or daughter is 100% suitable for those schools and he must fully support the application. This is very important because these schools will be in contact with your child's current school and ask for references and letters of recommendation.

Even in one of the prospectuses, I read that the school will ask for reference letters from the headmaster and, if there are several applicants from that school, the headmaster will be asked to prioritise his candidates.

At this stage I would like to tell you a little bit about the feeder school concept.

Each senior school usually has a very good, ongoing relationship with a few specific prep schools. It is proven by years of experience that students coming from those prep schools satisfy the requirements and fit very well when they move to these senior schools.

Some prep schools are feeder schools because of their physical closeness or, in some cases, the students coming from those prep schools consistently match the academic and behavioural requirements of that senior school.

Headmasters' and headmistresses' interpersonal and networking skills are very important too. Some of them have close, ongoing relationships with senior schools' headmasters and registrars at a more personal level. Therefore, when they support a pupil's application, their opinions are taken into account.

I heard that, in some circumstances such as things going unexpectedly wrong in the exam or interview, a call from the feeder school's headmaster might change the outcome.

So be aware of the feeder school concept and the

importance of the headmaster's role in these assessments.

CHAPTER 15

School Visits

After the meeting, my husband, Teoman, and I agreed to register Sarp for Westminster, St Paul's, King's College Wimbledon and City of London schools.

I arranged visits for those four schools.

When visiting schools, you can either book to join group tours or, for some schools, you can arrange individual private tours. At Westminster, King's College Wimbledon and City of London schools we joined the group tours and at St Paul's we had a private tour.

One day, I was talking to one of the mums at school about the schools we had visited and she told me that she had had a private tour at Westminster School. When I learnt about this, I arranged a private tour for St Paul's School which was the last school we were going to visit.

I am not sure if a private tour is better than the group tour. First of all, I don't think it is important at the selection process and secondly, private tours could be little bit intimidating both for you and your child. A senior person from the school spends almost an hour with you. He takes you around the school and tells you little, interesting stories about the rooms, old headmasters or objects at the school. In theory, it sounds good but, in reality, it is very stressful because you feel that it is an opportunity for you and for your child to impress that person. But at the same time you see your child getting bored and fidgeting or picking their nose. Also, you know that your child should ask questions and engage with that person but most likely they don't.

CHAPTER 16

Is Tutoring Necessary?

I n our meeting at school we were told that no extra work was necessary. I had doubts about this,
because in the past many kids were advised by the
school to apply to top academic schools but then
some of them who relied only on school teaching
didn't get in. So, I decided to take control into my
own hands.

I knew that Sarp was doing well but, without a private tutor to talk to, it is very difficult to understand
where your child actually stands in the process. I am
not saying that all kids need private tutoring but if
the child is not a genius, it definitely helps you and
your child. Of course, you should always find an
experienced tutor who knows what he/she is doing.

I had friends whose children had gone through the same thing the previous year. I asked them how to find the right tutor and they told me about a company that provided private tutors, mock exams, interview practices etc. The reason I am not mentioning the company's name here is because I wasn't happy with them at all. I definitely knew more about the process than they did and, for me, the worst part was that some of the advice I was given by their specialists was completely wrong. So you must work with the right company and tutor. You should talk to people and judge them for yourselves. Not everyone who says he/she is an expert in this field is an expert. Be careful!

I called the company and booked an appointment. In our first meeting, we talked about different schools, their exam procedures and the differences between the 11+ test, 13+ test and the 11+ pretest. They then suggested a tutor.

In reality, Sarp was already very good at maths, verbal and non-verbal reasoning and comprehension. All the Bond exercises he had done through the years were paying off.

The thing he needed to improve was creative writing.

We asked the tutor to focus mainly on English. We were worried about English because we were not native speakers as parents and we always spoke Turkish at home.

But actually, Sarp was already very good at English too. From a very early age, he loved reading. He read everything he could find. I encouraged him by reading with him and spending time at libraries and book stores together when he was little. After that, I didn't need to buy many books because, luckily, DPL had a very good library and, more importantly, a great librarian, Mrs. Fletcher.

Mrs. Fletcher had already read most of the books in the library and knew each boy and their taste in books very well. She gave recommendations to the boys and she organised book clubs at school. Sarp, and even I, benefited from her experience a lot. She recommended so many great books to Sarp and, after a while, he became the best borrower from the school library.

We lived a long way from school and spent long hours driving to and from school every day. One unpredictable advantage of this was that Sarp always read during our school journeys. Sometimes, it took just one day for him to finish his book. On average he used to read ten to thirteen books a month. He still does. If he can't find anything he enjoys to read, he re-reads the books he has already read.

The lessons with the tutor were going well. But the tutor was young and she was missing practical experience in exam procedure. The company suggested another tutor. This one was a very experienced, middle-aged guy who had worked as a headmaster in schools both in the UK and Latin America. He suggested some online websites to us, such as BOFA 11 plus and IXL.

BOFA 11 plus was very helpful. Sarp did all his preparation for the exams in maths, English, verbal and non-verbal reasoning by concentrating on the exercises and tests on this website. Apart from that he studied mental maths through Schofield and Sims exercise books.

The tutor had also recommended the IXL website for maths. The website is actually very useful for all ages if you would like to concentrate on learning subject by subject. Once you become a member, it doesn't matter how many children you have, and what their ages are, you have access to all the subjects for different year groups.

It was a great resource but I didn't use that website

for Sarp. It was much more suitable for my younger son, Derin. Even today I keep my membership so whenever Derin finds any subject in maths difficult, we go to that website and he practices on that specific subject. I know there is Mathletics too but, for me, the format for IXL is much more practical from a parent's point of view. Also, at later stages, I used an application called Squeebles to teach Derin times tables, division and fractions. That application was also really good and engaging.

Anyway, the new tutor was very experienced and he had some great recommendations but when it came to real teaching he had an attitude problem. Most of the time he didn't come to the lessons, without even notifying me, and when I contacted him about the situation, four out of five times, the excuse was that he had a flat tyre. So, after two months, I decided to cease lessons with this tutor.

I wasn't too worried about not finding the right tutor because I knew that Sarp was already good enough academically and he didn't need tutoring anyway.

But, at the same time, I am very happy that I got help from private tutors because, even though academically they couldn't add much to Sarp, they helped me to understand the process, introduced me to online teaching tools and shared their know how with me. So I felt more in control.

Another reason that Sarp didn't need much tutoring was because both my husband and I came from very academic backgrounds and we were able to help Sarp at home with all the subjects. This may not be the case for all parents.

CHAPTER 17

Creative Writing

Now, when I say Sarp was good at all subjects, there was one small exception to that. Contrary to the other subjects, he was quite bad at creative writing. To me it was very strange because when I thought about the number of books he read and how much he loved books, I would have expected him to be able to write naturally but he was really struggling. He had difficulty in imagining.

This was not something either my husband or I could help him with. Firstly, English was not our first language and secondly, both of us came from technical, engineering and finance backgrounds without much emphasis on imagination and creativity. Therefore, we struggled with our imagination more than Sarp.

One more time, I found another tutor for Sarp

just to teach him creative writing. She was great. She used role play and fun games to help Sarp to release his creativity.

The problem was, after three months, Sarp was still doing very badly. There wasn't even the slightest improvement in his writing.

Then one day, just one month before his pre-tests, something happened. He started to produce great pieces of writing full of creativity, great descriptions and very original ideas. I don't know how it happened exactly, but I am very glad that it did.

Initially, he was surprised at himself too but, at the same time, he really enjoyed being good at writing and I could see how confident and proud he felt. The writing homework that used to take a very long time with poor quality started to take only fifteen minutes with amazing imagination and descriptions.

I think creative writing is something you learn once in your life and you never forget it again. Because it is the process of setting your imagination free. Since that day, Sarp enjoyed writing and never looked back. Even today, when I read his essays, I am amazed by the originality of his ideas and I am so glad he has learnt to express himself in writing.

CHAPTER 18

Back to Kumon with Derin

While Sarp was studying full on for his tests, Derin was having the time of his life at school.

He was very happy at the nursery. The first year was part-time but in the second year his class became full-time like the rest of the school. The following year, the school decided to cease the part-time afternoon session because the hours were not convenient for parents. I think it was just Derin's and our luck that the school had decided to experiment with part-time afternoon sessions the previous year.

At nursery, children from each class would do different activities such as pieces of writing, pictures, models etc and display them outside the class on the walls. I noticed that, in Derin's class, with a couple of exceptions, most of the written work was not of the same standard as the work that was being done by other classes.

The majority of kids coming from part-time afternoon sessions were academically behind their peers in the full-time sessions.

In my opinion, there might have been two reasons for that. To start with, their first year at school was part-time. Therefore, they didn't have as much time for learning as the other children.

The other reason, as I discovered at a later stage, was that some of the kids including Derin, in the part-time class, had some difficulty in their assessments anyway.

So, I guess they were not as ready as the other kids for school from the beginning and, on top of that, they had less learning time at school in the first year compared to their peers.

After the first two years in nursery, Derin started Year 1. In Year 1, new classes were formed by mixing boys from different classes.

When the academic year started, I immediately noticed that Derin was quite behind academically compared to the other kids in his class. It didn't take me long to learn that the majority of children from the part-time class were in the same situation as Derin in their new classes.

At DPL, teaching in class is quite personalised. Kids with different abilities get different levels of work. If a child is doing well academically, he will get extension work and if he is not doing well enough, then he gets support. If a kid needs support, he is given one to one teaching regularly in the subjects in which he needs to improve without any additional cost to the parents.

DPL has a great approach. It assures parents that children learn at different paces, especially when they are young, and kids are given the necessary teaching at the right level.

I heard from mums who had children at different schools, that some very academic schools put a lot of pressure on parents if the kids don't do well academically. Sometimes, parents are even asked to move their child to another school because they think that he or she can't cope with the academic level at that school, even though those kids went through an assessment and interview process to get into the school.

Luckily, at DPL, the kids who are not doing well academically are not written off like some of the other schools in London. It is a very crowded school and you get all kinds of kids with many different interests and abilities. So it is not all about league tables.

I wasn't at all worried. Whenever there was a parents' evening to provide feedback about pupils, I was told Derin gets support academically but, apart from that, he is also a very kind, social and playful child. He not only plays with kids but also loves chatting with adults too.

Also, after my big failure with Sarp, I didn't want to make the same mistake again with Derin by pushing him academically.

So, I helped Derin with his homework at home and, apart from that, I left all education matters to the school.

In the meantime, I also noticed that kids were fully aware of other pupils' academic levels in the class. After a while they all knew who was doing well and getting extension work and who needed support.

I really didn't want to be involved this time but also I saw that the academic gap between kids getting support and extension work was getting wider and wider. I didn't want Derin to think he was not as good as the others and lose his confidence.

In my opinion, if a child is good at something, it is easier for him to like that subject and the more confident he feels, the better he will do in that area. If he is not doing well at something, he starts not liking it then it is more difficult to break that perception.

Even though I didn't want to intervene, I realised that I had to do something quickly and effectively to restore Derin's confidence.

This time I didn't rush into anything. I thought about my options. Derin was having difficulty with reading, writing and numbers. Basically everything academically for his age.

I had a serious think about it and, even though it had turned into a disaster before with Sarp, I decided to start doing Kumon with Derin.

This time I waited until the Easter holiday. Before the holiday I booked an appointment with the local Kumon centre for an assessment and I specifically told the lady that it was impossible for Derin to come to the centre every week. Instead, I suggested that I take the new worksheets and return the old ones myself. I agreed that he could come in from time to time for assessment of his level.

He was assessed and then given enough worksheets for the whole Easter holiday and we travelled to our summer house in Bodrum, Turkey, for three weeks.

In Bodrum, every morning we had our breakfast and afterwards we sat together as Derin did one maths and one English worksheet. In total it took one hour every day. After that he was free for the whole day. This wasn't very difficult for him because while he was doing his Kumon worksheets, Sarp was studying for his tests too. I noticed that even after couple of days he started to progress in both subjects.

When we returned to London, I continued doing Kumon with him for two more weeks but only one subject a day. Then we stopped completely because school and Kumon together was too much.

After a short while, there was another parents' evening for Derin. In that meeting, Derin's teacher told us that he had improved massively in the last two months and no longer needed support in either English or maths.

In my opinion, Kumon is a brilliant system for young kids, both for English and maths, as long as you make sure you take it easy and don't pressure the child with school and Kumon at the same time.

At later ages, kids can still benefit from Kumon in English by learning new vocabulary and developing their comprehension skills but I found maths Kumon too repetitive in that, in my opinion, no one needs to do that many exercises to grasp a subject.

After couple of months it was the summer holiday. I went back to the Kumon Centre and had Derin assessed again and collected my supply of worksheets for the whole summer holiday.

Again, we went to our summer house in Bodrum. I tried to do Kumon with Derin every day but this time I wasn't that strict. If we had other plans for the day or went away we skipped Kumon on those days.

After the summer holiday, Derin started to get extension work, both in English and maths.

CHAPTER 19

11+, 13+ Tests and 11+ Pretest

During the whole senior school exam preparation, the most difficult thing for me was to understand the differences between the 11+ test, 13+ test and the 11+ pretest.

For a long time, I thought that the 11+ test and the 11+ pretest was the same thing. Even after I learnt that they were different, I still wasn't sure which one Sarp was supposed to take. And, even after I understood which one was better for Sarp, I was still not sure about what the next step should be if he was, or wasn't, successful in those tests.

Here, I would like to share with you the differences, advantages and disadvantages of these tests.

Firstly, the test you choose will depend on which school your child is currently in.

If it is a school that continues up to eleven-years-old, then you have no choice but to find another school for your child after eleven and your child should definitely take the 11+ test to continue his education.

If it is a school that continues up to thirteen-years-old, then you have four options.

Your child takes the 11+ test and, if he is successful, he will change school the next academic year, before their current school ends, aged thirteen. If your son takes this test for Westminster and St Paul's schools, that means you have to register him for Westminster Under and St Paul's Juniors. If he is successful, he will start studying at Westminster Under and St Paul's Juniors when he is eleven-years-old, not the senior schools.

The good thing is, if your child is successful in the 11+ test, you don't need to worry about the 13+ test or CE exams. Even if he needs to pass CE at thirteen, you would assume that the school prepares its students for the exam.

If your child is not successful, they can still stay at their current school until they are thirteen-years-old and take the 13+ test for other schools then.

The drawback is that most schools in London

finish at age eleven. Therefore, the competition is fierce. The bright students who might have a chance of getting into those schools aged thirteen may not even be called for the interview if they take the 11+ test. Lately, some schools have increased their intake at the 11+ tests to tackle this issue.

Some academically very selective schools, such as Westminster, St Paul's, King's College Wimbledon, City of London, Eton, Tonbridge, Winchester etc, have pretests that your son needs to take aged eleven. They are called 11+ pretests. Even though your son will not start going to those schools until the age of thirteen, he must pass all the tests and the interviews in Year 6, when he is eleven, for him to be offered a conditional place to start those schools when he is thirteen.

The condition is, in Year 8, your son must either pass the school's scholarship exam or get the minimum mark in all the required subjects at the CE exam. Required minimum marks vary from school to school. For example, Westminster School asks for a minimum of 70% in maths, English, French, Latin, science, history, geography and religious studies. For City of London School, the pass rate is 65%.

I was told that passing the CE exam was not an issue at all. It is very, very rare for someone to manage to get a conditional offer from those schools and then fail at CE.

The biggest advantage of taking the 11+ pretests is that your child will have a better chance of succeeding as there will be less children competing for the places.

I wasn't really sure which exam was more suitable for Sarp (11+ test or 11+ pretest) and, after attending an open day at Westminster School, I asked this question to the registrar. She told me that my son would definitely have more chance if he took the 11+ pretest rather than the 11+ test.

If your child is successful in the 11+ pretest, you end up having a very confident and proud child and you will also know two years in advance which school your child will attend, so that you can relax.

If your son is not successful then it is still not the end of the world. He can wait until the age of thirteen and take the 13+ test for other schools.

Some schools only test children at eleven for 11+ entry and at thirteen for 13+ entry. They don't have pretests at eleven. For example, Dulwich College is one of them. If the child is successful in this exam at thirteen then he doesn't need to take the CE exam.

This was my backup strategy for Sarp.

Your child may take both the 11+ test and 11+ pretest. So if they are successful at the 11+ test and manage to get into the school they want, your child can change their school the next academic year. If they are not successful at the 11+ test but pass the 11+ pretest they can stay at their current school and take CE exam aged thirteen and then start studying at that school. Or, if your child is not successful at either of them, they can wait for the 13+ tests for other schools in Year 8.

This strategy may not work for all schools because some of them only allow your son to take one of the exams. But, for some schools such as St Paul's, you can register your son for the exams at St Paul's Juniors and St Paul's School separately. Even though the exam and interview dates are very close, they won't clash.

I thought about this strategy and I wanted to register Sarp for both exams but then our circumstances changed and it didn't make sense for Sarp to take the 11+ tests. So he only took the 11+ pretests.

CHAPTER 20

Life is Full of Surprises!

L ife is full of unexpected twists and turns. We plan things very carefully and seriously but, sometimes, things turn out completely differently than we expect. Years ago, Teoman, my husband, had worked for Banco Santander in London. He had a Brazilian boss whom he liked working with. Years later, he returned to Brazil and set up a hedge fund there. They always kept in touch. A couple of times he asked Teoman if he would consider working with him. Teoman didn't even think about it in the beginning.

One day, Teoman received an invitation from his old boss to go and visit their office in Brazil. It was just a short trip that would take four days. I knew how Teoman loved living in London and for me his trip to São Paulo was just for touristic purposes. On the second day of his visit, I received a call from Teoman telling me how he liked the office environment there. And when he called me on the third day he told me that he had visited a school in São Paulo and it was very impressive.

When Teoman came back from the trip, he was so excited. He had been asked to go and work in São Paulo for two years and then return back to London to set up the London office.

He asked me what I thought. In my opinion, two years was not a long time and it would bring dynamism to our lives. Also, I knew that Sarp would have more chance if he took the 11+ pretests rather than the 11+ exams. So, if he was successful in those exams he was going to change school when he was thirteen anyway and it would give us the exact two years to have this adventure. If he was not successful in the pretests, I knew that it would be really good to get away from London for a while to forget about everything and get refreshed after putting ourselves into such a stressful situation.

Before making up our minds completely, we wanted to talk to our headmaster to ask his opinion on

whether the children and I should move to São Paulo for two years or if it would be better for Teoman
to go and for me and the boys to stay in London.
Because, even though I liked the idea of having a
two-year adventure, it wouldn't be very easy to organise everything; all the logistics and disruption to
the way we live, the school and friendships just for
two years.

We arranged an appointment. At the meeting we
told him that we were very hesitant and worried
about disrupting Sarp's and Derin's lives for such
a short period of time and asked him his opinion.
Our headmaster was very positive and enthusiastic
about the move. He told us that he fully supported
the move as a whole family. In his opinion, learning
about a different culture and another language was
one of the best things that could happen to kids and
we should grab this opportunity both for ourselves
and for our children.

He, himself, had had a similar opportunity when
his children were around the same ages as ours.
They had moved to Japan for a while and it had
turned out to be a great experience for the whole
family.

He added that he would call the schools where

Sarp was going to take the exams and ask them if it was possible for him to take a different exam in Brazil, rather than the CE exam, in case he got into those schools.

He also assured us that Sarp and Derin would be accepted to DPL when we decided to return to London. So we needn't have worried about it at all.

When we left his office, we were smiling and very excited about the move.

People may not understand how important the role of the headmaster or headmistress is until they need their help. After all my experience of the senior schools admission process and our move, now I know that they are the people who have the power to change a school for better or worse.

So I would encourage you to research the head of the school before you decide what school is suitable for you and your children.

CHAPTER 21

What Now?

When people move abroad for work, usually they have a time limit in their minds but, in the majority of cases, they end up staying longer.

I was concerned because Sarp had been preparing for the exams, full on, for a long time. I wasn't sure whether we should carry on with the preparation as if nothing was happening. Studying for those exams required a lot of extra work and dedication both from Sarp and me and I wasn't sure what was going to happen if he managed to get into those schools.

I am a person who focuses on the steps to reach a target, rather than the target itself, and I always prefer to have many options available to me so that I can be in a position to decide what I want at the end, even if this means much more work.

In the end, I decided to carry on. Teoman and I

decided that he would move to São Paulo first and we would join him after all Sarp's exams and interviews had finished.

CHAPTER 22

Rules and Requirements

In the meantime, our headmaster contacted Westminster, St Paul's and King's College Wimbledon schools to clarify our situation.

King's College Wimbledon was the most helpful. We were told that if Sarp was made a conditional offer, they could send a special test to Sarp's school in Brazil to be administered there instead of the CE exam.

Westminster School told us that it is recommended that pupils attend a school in the UK two years prior to their entry to Westminster to prepare them for the CE exam and Sarp must definitely take the CE exam in the UK.

St Paul's School was the most rigid. According to

their admission rules, kids must definitely attend a UK school in the two years prior to their entry to St Paul's School and there was no flexibility on their side at all. I understood that they wanted children coming from the British education system but in Sarp's case he had studied in the British education system all the way from nursery and even if he managed to get into St Paul's, it was impossible for him to study there because of the one and a half year gap. I didn't think it was fair.

In light of this information, it would have been unrealistic to expect St Paul's School to bend its rules for Sarp. However, with me being the kind of person who pursues everything until the end, we decided to carry on as usual with the preparation for all those four schools as if nothing had changed.

CHAPTER 23

Selection Process

I don't know how the senior school selection process is in every other country in the world but, I think the system in the UK is very complicated and confusing. The whole examination process is different from school to school.

For example, City of London Boys School has its own exam papers in English, maths, verbal and non-verbal reasoning and also your son is asked to write a creative writing piece on a given subject. The whole examination takes at least four hours, and tests are administered one after another. If the child is successful in those tests then he is called for an interview at a later stage.

King's College Wimbledon, has exactly the same process.

The process for Westminster and St Paul's schools

is a little different. They have a common computer-based exam first that your son will sit in maths, English, verbal and non-verbal reasoning at his current school. The advantage of this is that your son doesn't need to go to another school and he takes the tests in an environment with which he is very familiar. Also, schools usually administer one subject a day within school time, therefore, kids spend one hour each day on the exams rather than sitting in an exam environment for four hours uninterrupted.

Before these computer-based exams, I gave Sarp lots of advice about test strategies. The most important point was to skip the questions he didn't know without spending too much time on them and to come back to those questions later on, after finishing the whole test.

How inexperienced I was and how very little I knew!

After his first exam, Sarp told me that, in the computer-based test, there was no going back so, basically, if you don't know the answer you have to make a guess right away.

If the child is successful in these computer-based tests, he will then be called for extra written exams and the interview at Westminster and St Paul's schools.

When potential pupils go for the interview, initially they are again given short English and maths papers, this time paper-based, and a creative writing task. After the poor kids have finished these extra exams, they are then interviewed.

Sarp hasn't taken the exam for Eton but I know from other children that Eton has a computer-based test too, which is very tricky. Obviously, Eton does not only assess children's English and maths ability but also wants kids with high intelligence as well.

In any case, Sarp didn't have any difficulty in passing all the exams for all four schools he had applied to.

CHAPTER 24

Interview Preparation

For me, the interview stage was the trickiest part of all the stages of assessment.

I decided not to do any preparation for the interviews until Sarp had passed the exams and was called for interview.

Instead of interview practice, I did something else. For four months prior to the exams, I took Sarp to a great many exhibitions, museums, concerts, plays, talks, monumental buildings and different neighbourhoods in London. Since he had already finished the academic preparation much earlier, well before the exams, we had enough time to allocate to his intellectual development.

In this process, again, DPL helped me a lot. At the

school there is a programme called Prep+, the aim of which is to develop the students intellectually. The school selects exhibitions, plays, dance shows, concerts, musicals, sports events and talks that are suitable for kids and buys a certain number of tickets for those events. Students or parents can access the social calendar through the school's website and sign up for the events and pay directly.

On the day or evening of the event, a school bus takes the children and parents there altogether with some of the teachers and when it finishes, the school bus brings everyone back to school.

You, the whole family, or even outside school friends, can accompany your child to these events or they can go alone.

The good thing is, as there are many kids joining these events from school, your son will have his friends with him and he will enjoy the activity more.

Also at DPL, there is the Leake Lecture Series every Wednesday after school. Experts come each week and talk about a different subject. The subjects cover a very wide variety from astronomy to history and from how to make fireworks to how to care for premature babies.

These lectures and Prep+ events provided a great

way to develop Sarp intellectually.

Derin also accompanied his brother to many of these events and talks. Some of them were very interesting for him too, or if it was something he found boring he happily fell asleep.

In the beginning, Sarp didn't like the idea of going to serious talks or concerts every week. He preferred to stay at home and play computer games. Very surprising!

But after a while those events and talks became part of our lives and Sarp became quite enthusiastic about them. Of course, he enjoyed some of them more than others but, overall, he was excited about the different events.

Those four months were very educational for me too. It helped me to get to know my sons better in a way that I hadn't experienced before and showed me that education outside the school is at least as important as education in school.

The key here is just to enjoy the activities together and let the kids talk about them. If their opinions are positive that's great. If they are negative that's okay too. They have opinions and they manage to express them. That's the important part.

I should admit, some of the talks and events were

really boring. In those cases, during the event or when it finished, we looked at each other with silly, giggling faces and went to eat pizza or ice cream to cheer us all up. While we were eating we talked about how boring it had been and how desperately we had wanted it to end and speculated about the situation. Boring events were the ones we remembered and talked about over and over again and they made us giggle whenever we remembered them.

Also, we had a few bizarre situations too. One of the events was a Classical Film Music Concert at the Royal Festival Hall. Derin was accompanying us and in the fifth minute he fell asleep. Not only did he fall asleep, but he also started snoring. So we decided to leave early. And for the rest of the week we talked about it and laughed. Derin was very happy to be a part of these events too.

CHAPTER 25

Interview Practice

I waited until I received letters calling Sarp for interview. Finally, they arrived one by one. He had gone through to the interview stage for all four of the schools where he was assessed.

At the DPL meeting for future schools, we had been told that the school was going to arrange mock interviews to prepare kids for the interviews but nothing was initiated until I asked them. Even then, Sarp had only one mock interview two days before his first interview date. I am not sure how helpful it was.

I didn't know what to expect from the interview at all. I checked the Internet, read all the blogs and chats to find out anything useful about what could be asked at the interviews.

It was so broad. Basically, it could be about anything from maths, geography, English, history and science to their personal interests or family lives.

For the academic part there wasn't anything more we could do.

First of all, Sarp and I sat together and read all the prospectuses for those schools. We tried to understand the differences between them and what kind of person would fit into those schools.

Secondly, we came up with different topics that could be asked:

1. Introducing himself.
2. Sarp's current school. What he likes, what he doesn't like about his school. What he would change.
3. Subjects he likes and dislikes and why.
4. The book he is reading right now. His favourite book and the book he didn't like at all.
5. His favourite authors.
6. His hobbies.
7. What his friends think about him and how they would describe him.
8. What he expects from a good friend.
9. How he spends his weekends and holidays. His favourite holiday.
10. Fantasy questions. Such as; what he would do if he had £1,000,000 or what super power he would

want and why or which animal he would choose to be and why.

11. Current affairs. Sarp tried to be up to date with what's going on in the world by watching BBC Newsround every day.

12. What he wants to do when he grows up.

13. Why he wants to go to that school.

14. Which other schools he is applying to. I still don't know the right answer to this question. I am not sure what they expect to hear. My feeling is they don't like to learn that the child is applying to too many schools. Also, I am not sure if the answer has real importance on the decision process but all four schools asked Sarp this question. So there must be a reason.

15. What is his first choice of school. Our strategy was to tell each interviewer that their school was Sarp's first choice and we found some specific, positive points about each school to support this decision.

I knew from the beginning that Sarp wanted to get into Westminster School and that was his first choice. But it needs a lot of courage to be honest when the child is answering this question. Also, if I were the interviewer I might think I am wasting a very valuable place on someone who is not genuinely interested in the school. So, even though it is not nice to ask your child to lie, I still think that not being completely honest in respect of your first choice of school is the least risky option.

16. At the end, your child will be asked if he or she has any questions they would like to ask. Obviously, they should ask at least one or two questions specific to that school.

CHAPTER 26

Interviews

I would like to tell you a little bit about one of the events I attended when I was in Brazil.

The school my sons studied at in São Paulo organised a UK and US Universities Fair. There were people from Imperial and King's Colleges too. They talked about their universities and compared the selection process for the UK universities with the selection process for the US universities. The lady from Imperial College said, 'In the US, the schools are after the students' hearts whereas in the UK, schools are after the students' brains.'

In my experience this statement completely reflects the interviews Sarp had.

After all those hours of assessing the kids in maths, English, verbal and non-verbal reasoning, I assumed that the interviews would focus more on Sarp's personality. But I was wrong again.

The interviews were dominated by challenging the kids academically with little emphasis on them personally. I think they were trying to understand how their brains worked.

The only exception was Westminster School.

For the interview at Westminster School, Sarp was asked to bring an object that was important to him and he was expected to talk about it. Also, apart from that, all the questions in the interview were targeted at getting to know Sarp personally, such as which book he was reading right now, his favourite book and his ideal weekend.

Before the interview at St Paul's, he again was tested in English, maths and creative writing. The subject for the creative writing piece was 'If you have to choose either writing a short story or a short play, which one would you choose, why?'

At the interview he was shown a photo of an island that was taken from very high up and he was expected to brainstorm about what kind of place it could be; whether he thought any humans live there. He was also asked, "If there is gravity, then why don't clouds fall?" Another question was, "How are volcanoes created?" He was also asked questions from history about King John. He was asked about his favourite book, how his friends describe him and what he likes most about St Paul's School.

There are a couple of differences with St Paul's School's 11+ pretest interview process.

First of all, there are no specific interview dates. Children might be called for the interview anytime from January to September in a nine month time frame. I am guessing that they arrange the interview dates according to how well the kids do in the exams. The better your son does in his exams, the earlier his interview date will be. Almost one week after the interview you get the result. Therefore, it is likely that more places will be offered to the ones who did well in the exams. Sarp was called for the interview at the very beginning of their interview period. So I assumed he did very well in the exams.

Secondly, at St Paul's, parents are interviewed too. Of course, they don't call it interview, but it kind of is. Your son is taken to a room for his interview and parents are taken to another room to chat with a senior person from school. I had no idea what to expect from that meeting and my husband was away so I attended alone. I was asked to talk about Sarp, then I was given information about the school.

After Sarp's interview finished, we exchanged rooms. I went to see the person who had just interviewed Sarp, and Sarp came to the room to meet the guy with whom I had just had a meeting.

Sarp's interviewer gave me feedback about his interview with Sarp. He told me that in the beginning Sarp was nervous but afterwards he became more relaxed. Also, he told me that it was great that Sarp was not prepped for the interview beforehand. I felt that he was very surprised by this. I was surprised with this comment too, because I thought that we did quite a bit of preparation for the interview. But he told me, some kids are so intensely prepped by their tutors that they are afraid of saying anything wrong.

Now, this sounds like a positive comment but I have lived long enough in the UK to be able to distinguish positive structured sentences with positive meanings and positive structured sentences with negative meanings. My feeling was that it was going to be much easier for the school to offer a place to Sarp if he was like the other prototype boys.

Towards the end of the meeting, the interviewer told me that I could arrange another interview date if I was interested. So, obviously, he was not 100%

convinced with Sarp but at the same time he saw his potential and wanted to give Sarp one more chance to truly understand him. I really appreciated that. It is good to see that the school makes every effort to really understand the kids. Also, I like the idea of parents being a part of the process. It adds transparency to the whole process and lets you understand the reasons behind their positive or negative decision.

Exam results are very clear, there is nothing to argue with, but interviews are very tricky because schools might be looking for different qualities in children and parents don't know what these qualities are. Therefore, from a parents' point of view, it is very difficult to understand why your child is successful or not at an interview. Usually, if the result is positive and the child is offered a place, parents are so happy that they may not care about the reasons behind the decision. However, if the child can't get an offer and you think he or she really deserves a better result, you want to know the reasons for that decision and St Paul's interview process gives you an insight as to how they decide.

I didn't want to arrange another interview date for Sarp at St Paul's because I knew that the school was very strict about the condition of studying in a UK school in the two years prior to starting. We were moving to Brazil and it was impossible for us to fulfil that obligation. So I thanked him and we left. One week later we got the result. Sarp was on the waiting list for St Paul's School.

Almost one and a half years later, when Sarp was in Year 8, I received an email from St Paul's School asking for reserve list candidates to come for extra exams and interviews to decide the boys who were going to be transferred to the main list, but we declined this invitation since Sarp had already made up his mind and he was very happy with Westminster School.

At the King's College Wimbledon interview he was asked mental maths questions. He was shown a picture and he was asked to talk about what kind of story the picture tells him and again he was asked his favourite book and how many books he reads a month.

At the City of London interview, Sarp was asked mental maths questions. He was given a passage and asked questions about the passage and the vocabulary used. He was asked which book he didn't like at all and why. So, finally, the classic book I had specifically asked Sarp to read became useful in the end! The book Sarp didn't like was Carrie's War by Nina Bawden.

I know all four schools are very academic schools and they challenge the kids' ability by testing them for different subjects. But I believe the way the schools conducted their interviews gave us some insight to the real characters of those schools.

In my opinion, St Paul's, King's College Wimbledon and City of London Schools expect articulate pupils with an in depth knowledge in the areas the schools are interested in, whereas Westminster School wants children to demonstrate their passion and in depth knowledge in the areas the kids are interested in. I think this kind of approach allows kids to express their individuality and value their differences.

CHAPTER 27

Stress

F or me, the whole exam preparation was very stressful from beginning to end. It continued to build up and towards the end, during our preparations for the interviews, it was unbearable.

There were a few factors contributing to this.

First of all, my husband had already moved to Brazil and started working there. I was alone with the kids in London for the last seven months. I was the one who was solely responsible for Sarp's exam preparation on top of everything else.

Secondly, because of our move, there were so many issues that had to be sorted out, such as renting out our house, selling our car, going through every single item in the house to make sure we wouldn't store unnecessary things for two years, deciding what to take to Brazil and all the other tiny issues relating to the move.

Thirdly, we had decided to move abroad but the kids were not happy with this decision at all. They loved their school and friends and they didn't want to be separated from them. So I had to deal with the psychological side of the move too.

Socially, I was also very busy. Since we were leaving, I frequently got together with my friends for leaving drinks. I also organised big leaving parties both for Sarp and Derin separately.

From time to time, my friends asked me if I was excited about the move but, in reality, I didn't have even one moment to think about it. I just went with the flow. Every day I woke up with a 'to do' list and just focused on doing the things on it.

On top of that, my mum came from Turkey to help me with the move. My mum and I have always been very close. I talk to her on the phone at least three times a week if not every day. My kids adore her too. She plays with Sarp and Derin all the time when she is with us and she takes care of them when I go away on holiday with my husband. As a mum and daughter, we get on very well but, of course, there are some things that we don't agree with each other about.

She had never been a pushy mummy herself and she didn't approve of my efforts for the exam and interview preparations.

In her opinion, our life is too child-centric. She thinks parents sacrifice too much for their kids nowadays, but in return, they expect achievements from them. She believes it doesn't matter how much parents push them, kids will end up where they are supposed to be in life.

I really didn't know how to react to this comment. I always felt that I had the potential to do better in life if my parents had guided and pushed me little bit. I think that is the underlying reason behind me pushing my kids academically.

But maybe if my parents had done that I might have reacted adversely and wouldn't have benefited at all. It is true that, regardless of their age, most people learn and achieve things when they really want to, not when other people tell them to.

When I look at myself, I see a person who relies on herself in life rather than waiting to be saved by someone else and this makes me feel confident and in charge of my own life. Also, I know exactly what I want and what I don't want since I have always been the sole person responsible to take any action.

So I really don't know if me being a pushy mum will really help my children in the long run but I am trying to do my best for them like all other mums.

I was very stressed but I tried not to reflect this to Sarp. I could see how anxious he was about all those exams and interviews too. I tried so hard to ease his stress.

So many times he asked me, "What if I can't get into those schools?"

My answer was always same. I told him how lucky I was to have a son like him and how good he had been in this process all the way from the beginning to the end. He had done his best and there was nothing more we could have done. I also told him that if it happens, it happens but if it doesn't, it doesn't. It's not the end of the world. If he didn't get into one of those schools, Sarp would have continued with Dulwich College which was a great school anyway.

We had promised to buy him the latest PlayStation console after the exams. I told him that the present was for all his efforts. He was going to get it, regardless of being successful or not, as soon as the last interview finished.

I could feel that, under all those emotional stresses, I was nearing my melting point.

We got the first result from St Paul's. Sarp was on the waiting list there, as I expected. I wasn't worried because I knew St Paul's wasn't an option for us anyway.

The second letter came from King's College Wimbledon. In the interview, Sarp was told that he had done brilliantly in the exams. Also, according to Sarp's feedback, the interviews there had gone really well too. I was quite sure that Sarp was going to get an offer from King's.

King's College School Wimbledon was not our first choice but, at the same time, the school had approached our situation very positively by allowing Sarp to take a substitute exam in Brazil in case he was offered a place. So it was going to be very convenient for me if Sarp had got an offer from King's.

That morning, I was going to meet up with my close friends for coffee at Rocca, the cafe we always went to in Dulwich Village, after school drop off. Their kids and Derin were in the same nursery class. They were with me all the way from beginning to end and they knew how difficult the whole thing was both for Sarp and me.

When I met them in the morning I had just received the rejection letter from King's. As soon as

I sat at the table I gave them the news and I started crying. I couldn't control myself. I cried and cried and cried. I was crying, not because Sarp couldn't get into that school, but because I was the one who wanted Sarp to study at those schools. I blamed myself for all the extra work and pressure I had put on him for a year. I felt like I had wasted one year of my son's life because of my ambition. He was already a brilliant boy and he didn't need to prove that to anyone.

Also, all the additional pressure of moving abroad and leaving the people I like behind had got to me in the end too. My friends didn't want to leave me alone that day. But after crying continuously for two hours at the cafe, I needed to go home. I cried in my car all the way home. Then I called my husband and cried on the phone and after that I called my mum, who had returned to Istanbul, and cried some more.

Even though my mum hadn't supported my idea of preparing Sarp for these exams, she didn't make a single comment about it and tried to calm me down. She got very upset too, again, not because Sarp couldn't get into that school but because of the amount of pressure on my shoulders. As a mum as much as I wanted to take care of my boys, my mum wanted to take care of me too.

I knew I had to pull myself together before going to school to pick up Sarp and Derin.

I picked up Sarp and told him that King's Wimbledon hadn't made him an offer but it was their loss not ours.

I could see that he was disappointed but nothing compared to what I felt. Then I told him that I had arranged a sleepover for him at his best friend's house. His mood improved instantly. Kids are incredibly resilient compared to adults and they are not concerned with past or future. They have the gift of living in the now.

After couple of days, I contacted King's College School Wimbledon to receive feedback but I was told they could only give feedback to Sarp's headmaster and he should contact them personally. At the end we ended up not contacting the school at all.

One day before our move to São Paulo, we received a letter from City of London, offering a place to Sarp. I felt big relief!

I filled out the forms and prepared the cheque and gave them to one of my best friends in London. I told her to hang on to the envelope until I told her to post it, because we were still waiting to hear from Westminster School, the first choice for the whole family.

I have already told you, in the beginning of the book, what happened with Westminster School. Sarp got an offer from Westminster ten days after we moved to São Paulo.

After we received the result from Westminster School, I couldn't do anything for almost a week. Every day I received so many phone calls and emails from family members and friends who wanted to congratulate Sarp.

In the end, Sarp got offers from both Westminster and City of London schools. He was on the waiting list for St Paul's School. I believe if I had arranged the second interview as was suggested, he would most likely have got an offer from St Paul's too. He was rejected by King's College School Wimbledon and I still have no idea why.

CHAPTER 28

Life in São Paulo

Before moving to São Paulo, I was so busy that I didn't have any time to think or fantasize about our new life there. I think it is better not to have any expectations beforehand when you are starting something new. Because then, even the smallest nice thing is enough to make you happy.

I really needed a break from my over-pressurised London life and São Paulo gave me this opportunity.

The weather was beautiful. It was the best weather I had ever seen. The temperature was not too cold or hot. During the day sometimes it was sunny, sometimes rainy. It even hailed but the temperature was always warm. I loved it. I had lived in London for seventeen years and I couldn't understand why my mum made such a big fuss about the weather in London but apparently the weather makes a huge difference to people's lives and happiness.

Brazilian people are so relaxed. They never hurry for anything. Even if they are late, they don't rush. They also have huge tolerance towards other people. Even though poverty is a very big problem, people are genuinely happy. You don't see any Brazilian eating alone at a restaurant. At lunch breaks people go out for lunch with their colleagues and friends, never alone.

Football is one of the most important things in their daily lives. They love playing and talking about it. Being in Brazil during the World Cup was a great experience for the whole family.

Sarp hadn't wanted to move to São Paulo but as soon as we moved there, both Derin and Sarp easily settled into their new schools and lives. Sarp's teacher told me that Derin had seen her during break time and told her to treat Sarp very well because changing schools is much harder for older kids. I don't know who he got that from!

There was nothing not to like about their lives. We had chosen a British school for them and it was co-ed. This didn't make much difference in Derin's life but Sarp started combing his hair in the mornings!

At school, there weren't any school exams even for Sarp's year. The curriculum was the same as the UK curriculum but the emphasis was on preparing presentations and class work. Even Derin was supposed to prepare regular presentations about a variety of subjects. Neither Sarp nor Derin had much homework.

You might think that, after having such a relaxed academic life, kids wouldn't have much chance of going to good universities, but this isn't true. When we were there, many children got offers from very good universities all over the world and, apart from that, two pupils got offers from Cambridge and another three received offers from US Ivy League Universities including Harvard. So obviously the school was not doing badly academically.

On the first day of school, I went to pick Derin up from his class and his teacher told me that he needed to stay little bit longer since he was teaching the other kids to shake hands before leaving the class. One of the girls strongly objected to this idea. She said, "I don't want to shake hands. I want to hug my teacher, I want to kiss her." I also saw other kids in Sarp's age group hugging their teachers. It was a completely different atmosphere.

The school structure was different too. There were only two PE lessons during the week. The school day ended at 2.45 p.m. After that the school provided many free activities such as football, volleyball, basketball, swimming, frisbee, table tennis, chess etc and there were also musical instrument lessons that you had to pay for. Kids chose the ones they liked and stayed longer at school, depending on the activities they had selected. This approach gave the kids the opportunity to skip the activities they didn't like at all.

Of course, some kids were better than the others in those activities but they always played together without getting distributed into A, B, C, D, E, F and G teams. The school selected some pupils for the school teams for different activities and competed with other schools but at school, they always played in mixed ability groups.

Then I noticed how much Sarp enjoyed football. This gave him the opportunity to enjoy playing football without being labelled as E or F. Also playing with kids who have different abilities helped him to learn from others and get better.

When he was in Dulwich Prep London, he was

mainly in E and F teams. Once, he went up to the D team and joined a school match against another school, and he loved it, but the next week he was off sick and after that he could never make the D team again.

In Brazil, there is big security issue and, because of that, middle class people prefer to live in gated, secure condominiums. We did the same. Our condominium had an indoor and outdoor swimming pool, gym, playground and a small pitch to play football and basketball.

Every day, kids came home from school and did their homework, if they had any. Afterwards, they just went down and played with whoever was around. So my life changed completely. I didn't need to carry them from one activity to another. They just played downstairs. I didn't need to arrange constant play dates either. Kids from all ages got together and played together very happily. The best thing was I didn't need to be present while they were playing.

Brazilian kids were much more independent and confident compared to children in the UK. Since playtimes and get-togethers were mostly not arranged, and the places were secure, parents didn't need to be present with them at all. In Brazil, parents had lives too and they lived their own lives without worrying about their kids 24/7.

In my experience, in the UK parents mainly focus on their own kids and observe them to see if they need to improve at anything or if they are better than other kids at certain things. And that creates a lot of anxious parents about basically any topic related to their children, and children get more cautious about not doing anything wrong. When I was a kid, I played tennis, I played basketball and I swam but none of the mums watched us during our training which resulted in us enjoying the activities more and allowing us to be silly from time to time and have more fun.

Initially, it took me some time to adjust to this new mindset. I didn't find the amount of homework sufficient. I wanted to arrange some extracurricular activities for my children such as swimming or tennis. Because, even though we had two pools in our condominium, kids were just playing in the pool without swimming properly and I was so used to them learning things. But in reality, both Sarp and Derin were enjoying this lifestyle so much, they refused to go to any activities outside of their school and our condominium. I was worried for a while but then settled back into the relaxed Brazilian way of life.

Sarp and Derin were in the top sets for everything at their school there but, at the same time, I knew that the standards of the top sets in Brazil had nothing to do with the ones in DPL. Since Sarp had got into Westminster School and needed to take the CE exam, we were planning to return to DPL for his Year 8. A part of me just wanted to enjoy Brazil with its own conditions and another part of me thought that the boys would be quite behind when we went back to DPL. In the end, I chose to do nothing and we all had a great year!

When I say 'I did nothing', that is almost completely true. At their school, neither French nor Latin were taught. Therefore, I arranged for French and Latin tutoring once a week for Sarp via Skype.

CHAPTER 29

Competition, Competition, Competition

I am so proud of Sarp and I am very happy that he got the offer from Westminster School. I can also see how proud he feels about himself. He had never been an insecure child but after this, his confidence increased massively. It is lovely that he got the recognition he deserved after all his hard work. But at the same time, I know it was a very close call. Every year thousands of kids are prepared for these exams. Some study harder than Sarp but, in the end, only a handful of them succeed. I believe, in many cases, the difference between the ones that succeed and those who don't is minute. Sarp studied hard and he had the persona necessary for it but also I believe we were lucky too.

When I look at Sarp, I really believe he is Westminster material and he would not only thrive there, academically and personally, but contribute to the spirit of the school as well. However, in general, even though he got into Westminster School, I have doubts about the whole education and selection system in the UK.

In my opinion, it is too competitive from a very early age. The whole system is based on selecting the kids who have already been prepared for those things by their parents in advance. The system is result-oriented and schools and teams are after the children who can produce tangible results.

Of course, there are exceptions, but parents feel that, in order for their kids to succeed at school, they should either start those activities earlier than school or they should support them at home by additional work. I believe the kids who are doing well at music at school, are most likely taking private music lessons at home. Again the kids doing well academically at school are mostly pushed by their parents or have private tutors at home and the kids who are good at sports are most likely playing these sports outside the school as well. Parents pay school fees and, on top of that, they pay for all those additional activities and tutors to make sure their kids will be ready when the time comes for those activities at school.

This kind of approach takes a chunk of the teaching responsibility from schools and puts it on parents' shoulders. As parents, we are too anxious about our children and we try to be one step ahead of the school all the time. We know the system is full of exams and assessments starting from nursery, at the age of two, and if our kids don't show tangible differentiation from the beginning, the system will not be interested in their future potential.

This approach makes me question why good schools are good schools. Are they called good schools because they teach and guide the children so well or because they just select the kids who would do well whatever school they go to?

I know good schools have all those specialist teachers, state of the art facilities and numerous clubs but, in the end, they only accept special kids who have already proved themselves. They don't select regular students and then provide them with facilities and guidance to improve themselves. The schools' success is again measured by the exam results of their students and how many they send to well-known universities. I believe, even after selecting the readymade students who have been prepared intensely to study in those schools, they still rely on the support of those kids' parents to prepare them for future exams. At least, I feel that pressure on my shoulders. I have friends whose children study at the top senior schools in the UK and the children are still tutored privately to be able to keep their places in the top sets in the class or to be able to jump to better sets.

In the UK, kids start going to nursery at three-years-old, if not earlier. Since it is not easy to teach reading and writing to a normal three-year-old child, the schools start selecting the kids they can teach more easily. This creates a snowball effect and the main job of the whole system becomes preparing the kids for the next exam starting from a very young age.

From an academic point of view, I believe there is an age that most kids feel ready academically and trying to teach them things earlier puts a lot of unnecessary pressure on them and steals the most precious times of their childhood. It also puts pressure on their parents.

CHAPTER 30

Find Your Passion

As a mother, I want to do the best for my children. It is difficult for me to ignore the system completely even though I find it too competitive. On the other hand, I believe there is a healthy limit to how much parents can push their children. Each child is unique and it is the parents' job to guide their children by embracing their skills and qualities.

Sometimes parents, like me, target the most difficult schools to get into for their children because they think the harder a school is to get into, the better that school prepares their children for the future. They want their children to be equipped with the tools and techniques to help them to build successful and prosperous lives.

The world is changing so fast that I think it is important to remind ourselves that, in today's world, there are many different paths to successful and happy lives for our children.

There are still conventional jobs, such as doctors, teachers, lawyers, engineers, which require a high level of academic studies but also there are so many new areas of work and the emphasis on those areas are creativity, out of the box thinking and personality. Good grades and academic schools are not the only solution to a successful and prosperous life any more. When I look at the profiles of successful people, I see that they all have one thing in common. They are the ones who go after their dreams and not scared to pursue their passions in life.

Here, I would like to open a parenthesis and tell you about a documentary I watched while I was in Brazil. It is called Jiro Dreams of Sushi directed by David Gelb.

Jiro is a very old Japanese sushi master who has a renowned restaurant in Tokyo. He is so passionate for sushi that sushi becomes art in his hands. He is a recognised sushi chef in the world with three Michelin stars.

At one stage in the documentary, Jiro was asked to give a speech at the school he graduated from.

When he was preparing his speech, he wasn't sure what to say because, during his student years, he had never been a good student. And he didn't achieve his success because he did well at school. He just followed his dream. He found his passion and pursued it. Since it was a talk at school, he wanted to encourage children to study hard and do well at school but, in reality, the path that led him to his success was completely different.

I think schools should encourage pupils to think freely and be creative and help them to get prepared for the real life in front of them. Therefore, it is very important for our kids to have passions they can pursue. I believe that's the route to success and happiness in life today.

CHAPTER 31

Extracurricular Activities

I n the UK, children's education is complemented by extracurricular activities. A lot of emphasis is put on how beneficial they are for our children's personal, mental and physical development. I don't doubt that either. I believe that activities help children to find out more about themselves by discovering their skills and passions.

I believe that, if chosen and applied correctly, activities are a great tool for children to find new ways to express themselves. On the other hand, wrong application or overdoing them can easily harm our children, waste our time and our budgets.

I think there are a few points we should consider before and after starting the activities.

As a parent, I have experienced that it is very important to start these activities at the appropriate age. Sometimes parents think that the earlier their children start an activity the sooner they will improve at it. However, if the children are not ready, physically or mentally, then they might find the activity too challenging and be discouraged from it.

In the UK, children usually spend long hours at school. An ambitious number of extracurricular activities or too much time devoted to them, together with long school hours and homework might be overwhelming for children. Sometimes activities that start with genuine enthusiasm might turn into a burden if the child is having difficulty in juggling school, homework and extracurricular activities without any time to relax at home or play with friends. Being too occupied might also leave little or no time for your children to get bored and prevents them from releasing their creativity.

CHAPTER 32

Welcome Back to London

Towards the end of Teoman's second year in São Paulo, it had been nearly a year for me and the boys, since we couldn't join him until much later due to the exams and interviews, my husband got another job offer back in London. I knew it was a good opportunity for him and I knew the kids and I had to go back anyway because of the CE exam, but I really didn't want to return to London at all. London to me always meant studying hard, working hard and competing in every possible thing you can think of. And, on top of that, you must do everything in dark and freezing cold weather. Life in London really tests your physical and emotional strength.

We moved back to London shortly before the Easter holiday. Sarp and Derin were going to start the summer term of their Year 7 and Year 3. The week we arrived, there was a parents' consultation evening at school for Derin's year. Obviously, it was too soon for his teacher to have any opinions on him. So we arranged a meeting for three weeks' time, just before the school broke up for Easter.

In Brazil, Derin was doing really well academically and I didn't try to teach him anything extra even though I knew the standards at DPL were much higher.

At the meeting, I was told that Derin had settled back to his new class very easily and he was also doing well socially. However, academically he was a little behind. His teacher was very nice and positive and she assured me that Derin could easily close the gap. I had just started to think, there is nothing to worry about; I don't need to do anything extra, but then she mentioned that, in Year 4, the kids were going to be streamed according to their abilities in maths and they were going to be allocated to sets according to how well they were doing in the last term of their Year 3. I thought to myself, here we go again!

I knew from the feedback I got from his teacher, Derin could only be in the lower sets and once he was put into the lower sets, it wouldn't be easy for him to move up. Because, in my experience, the gap between sets gets wider and wider as time passes and it gets more difficult to catch up with the upper sets.

I knew that meant I had to do extra work with Derin so that he could catch up and I had to do it fast. And that evening Sarp came home saying that if he was going to take the scholarship exam for Westminster School, then he needed to learn Ancient Greek as well.

I thought to myself, Welcome back to London!

CHAPTER 33

The Challenge

When Sarp started Year 8, we realised that students aren't required to learn new information during that year, only consolidate what has been taught in Year 7 and revise for CE and scholarship exams. We knew that Sarp had gaps in his learning due to spending a year in Brazil. He had improved his football skills massively but missed the entire Year 7 curriculum in maths, English, history, geography, science, French and Latin.

At a meeting, parents were told that the school was going to evaluate and advise parents if their son should take CE or scholarship exams. At Westminster, the boys who get a Queen's Scholarship have to board. Sarp was never interested in boarding. That was the reason we had only applied to London day schools in Year 6. Attending a visit to see the boarding houses at Westminster School hadn't changed

Sarp's opinion either.

I also knew that the scholarship exam for Westminster was very hard. Considering that Sarp needed to do a lot of catching up in all subjects, the scholarship exam was very difficult and Sarp didn't want to board, our initial reaction was there was no need for Sarp to take the scholarship exams. Passing the CE exams was enough for him to secure his entry to Westminster.

For us, the only advantage of taking 'The Challenge', Westminster's scholarship exams, was that they were at the end of April, shortly after the Easter break, whereas CE exams were in June. The students who do well enough at 'The Challenge' still secure their places at Westminster even if they don't get a scholarship. So they can relax two months earlier than the students who are taking CE exams.

If they don't do well enough at 'The Challenge', then boys may be asked to take the CE exam in their weak subjects only or, if they under perform in all subjects, they may be asked to do full CE exams in June.

Sarp had returned to DPL in the last term of Year 7 and just before school ended he had end of year exams. Surprisingly, he did very well in those exams and when he started Year 8 he was put into the scholarship class at DPL. Parents were told that being in the scholarship class didn't mean the boy had to go through the scholarship exam. The school would track the students' progress and advise the parents nearer to the exams which one their son should take.

The teaching was quite personalised in the scholarship class. Students were taught separately depending on which schools they were planning to go to. If their future school required any additional subject, those boys were taught that subject separately or, in some cases, the boys didn't need to study some subjects at all. Westminster had an optional Greek exam so Sarp was taught Ancient Greek as well.

There were school exams just a couple of months before the scholarship exams to evaluate how the boys were doing. When Sarp told us his results, I was sure he wasn't up for scholarship exams. The grades I was used to hearing were much higher than these. Sarp assured me that his results were actually quite good compared to others in his class.

Two weeks later, there was a parents' evening. Each subject teacher told us how well Sarp did in his exams and that he should definitely go for the scholarship exams. When I questioned his low grades, I was told that the academic standard in scholarship exams is incredibly high and, actually, Sarp got quite decent marks on his exams.

I was proud of Sarp but then I knew how challenging scholarship exams were. At the same time, I noticed that Sarp was happy to be in the scholarship class and, even if he had to study a lot, he was willing to do it.

We decided to stay in London during the Easter break so that Sarp could study. I noticed a very big change in Sarp. Every day he woke up, had his breakfast and went to his room to study. He was very responsible and he completely took charge of it. There wasn't much I could help him with. He just needed my cooking skills and emotional support!

He had a very busy, three-day exam schedule, starting at 8.30 a.m. in the morning and ending at 5.00 p.m. in the afternoon. In three days he had exams in history, Latin, mathematics II, geography, mathematics III, English, science, French and Ancient Greek (optional). Also he had French dictation, French oral and an interview.

When Sarp woke up on the first day of the exams, I could see how nervous he was. Seeing him like that made me nervous too. For the whole day I kept looking at my watch and thought about him.

When I went to pick him up, I didn't know what to expect. Then I saw him coming out of school, with a smiley face. What a big relief! He immediately started chattering about the other boys he met, how they watched the older boys playing football and how nice the day was. Then he added that his exams had gone well too. He was looking forward to going back to school the next day to see his new friends.

I was enormously relieved not only because Sarp had had a nice day, but also because I felt reassured that Westminster was the right school for him. Even on one of the most stressful days, the school, teachers and other students could make Sarp feel at ease.

Five days later I received a call from DPL's headmaster. The school had received the results. He told me that Sarp had passed all his exams and his entry to Westminster was confirmed. We were all delighted with the result!

I had promised the boys a Chessington Theme Park visit after the exams. Both Sarp and Derin had deserved it for studying hard and behaving so well.

The next morning I drove the boys to school. The weather was beautiful. It was warm and sunny.

When we came to the bridge we always cross, on the way to school, we noticed that it was completely blocked by police. We perceived this as a sign for us to skip school and head directly to Chessington! We had a great day!

On the way back from Chessington, we were all very happy and cheerful. Then Sarp said, "I can't believe the exams are over," and Derin replied, "They are not over yet, now I must start studying!"

CHAPTER 34

Future Schools Evening Again

After the Easter break, DPL organised a 'Future Schools Evening' and invited Year 4 parents to provide information about the selection system and future school alternatives. I felt deja vu. I remembered going to another 'Future Schools Evening' four years earlier for Sarp with the exact same setting and I couldn't believe it was Derin's turn now.

When I gazed at the crowd before the event, I noticed many anxious-looking parents, whereas at the end of it, they all seemed calmer. Even I felt much better, even though I knew what was waiting in front of me!

CHAPTER 35

My Journey

My journey began thirteen years ago and still continues every day with new things to learn and share.

I truly enjoyed writing this book. It made me not only go back to my own childhood and appreciate my family again but also remember some of my forgotten memories of Sarp's and Derin's early years.

If you have read this book and don't agree with my way of thinking or doing that's fine, because this book only reflects my opinions and experiences. Parenting and priorities vary vastly from one person to another. The good thing is that we are all different as parents and our kids have different personalities too. Differences are what we should embrace.

If you have read this book and found that you and I have similar concerns in our lives, please use whichever part appeals to you and your family.

My intention is to continue updating this book as my children grow to see if what I am trying to do works for them in the long term and if they will turn into happy and confident individuals with prosperous lives.

Thank you.

ABOUT THE AUTHOR

Ayse Gunduz Sevin was born in Eskisehir, Turkey, in 1972. At the age of twenty-five she moved to London to pursue a career in finance and, since then, she has been living there on and off with her husband and two sons, Sarp, aged thirteen and Derin, nine.

Ayse is passionate about education, books and learning new things. She is the co-founder of Magnus Education London which provides a bespoke service for families from the UK, and elsewhere in the world, seeking advice regarding any aspect of their child's education.

Although she is obsessed with cappuccino, she can drink only one a day and it has to be before 1.00 p.m. Otherwise, she can't sleep at night!

Visit Ayse Gunduz Sevin's Website:

www.magnuseducationlondon.com

Contact Ayse Gunduz Sevin:

ayse.sevin@magnuseducationlondon.co.uk

RESOURCES

- The Good Schools Guide: Parent friendly school guide. Available both in published format and online.
- Gladwell, Malcolm. Outliers: The Story of Success. 1st ed. New York: Little Brown and Company, 2008.
- Gina Ford: Author of childcare books in the United Kingdom and a former maternity nurse.
- Anabel Karmel: Author of books in nutrition and cooking for babies, children and families.
- Kumon: Maths and English study programmes.
- Bond: Exercise books in maths, English, verbal and non-verbal reasoning.
- Bofa 11 Plus: Website for 11 plus exam preparation.
- Ixl: Website for practising maths and English online.
- Schofield and Sims: Educational publisher, providing books for teachers, parents and tutors.
- Mathletics: Online learning resource.
- Squeebles: Online learning application.
- BBC Newsround: Children's news programme.
- Jiro Dreams of Sushi: 2011 American documentary film directed by David Gelb.